Easy & Delicious Vegetarian Soup Recipes

31 Fresh, Fast and Soul-Satisfying Vegetarian Soup Recipes Almost Everybody Loves

Susan Scott

Table of Contents

Introduction

Soup – glorious soup! Few things satisfy the soup lover's palette like a piping-hot bowl of deliciousness. Nothing beats homemade soup made from scratch -- and with a whole lot of love.

Soup is comforting. It's nutritious and economical too. Most of all, homemade soup is soul-satisfying. What more could anyone ask than a hearty helping of **Potato Leek**, fresh-from-the-oven **French Onion Soup** with accompanying Caesar Salad, or a bountiful bowl of **Corn Chowder**, served up with fresh-baked bread?

Life can get complicated. That's why I like simple soups that taste great.

There's nothing too difficult here. Anyone can follow along and produce a quality meal that satisfies everybody – even picky eaters and committed carnivores too!

This small book gives you plenty of variety – with 25 different, vegetarian soups. Use these recipes to get started. You'll enjoy them as they are. But one of the great things about soup is that there are endless ways to change things up to suit your tastes – or the ingredients you happen to have on hand.

My focus has been creating tasty soups – without going off the charts with an excessive amount of butter, cheese and cream. I've included some butter and cheese in several recipes, but I've avoided cream altogether and only use milk in my cream soups and chowders.

You could also substitute all-purpose flour with whole wheat if you choose to. Low sodium broth cubes are another healthier option, though you may have to visit a health food store to find them.

Follow these recipes and you'll create wonderful meals that you, your family and guests will enjoy.

Happy Cooking!

Susan Scott

French Onion Soup

Ingredients:

¼ Cup Olive Oil
8 Medium to Large Onions (peeled, quartered lengthwise, then sliced thin)
2 Pinches Red Pepper Flakes
1½ Cups Dry White or Red Wine
5 Cups Water
2 Vegetable Broth Cubes
1 Small Loaf of Multigrain Bread or Crusty Baguette
2 Cups Grated Cheese (Swiss, Gruyere, Mozzarella – or a combination)
Fresh Ground Sea Salt and Pepper

Directions:

1. Heat olive oil in a wide sauce pan to medium. Add all onions and stir to coat with oil. Fry until onions are deeply browned, which typically takes 20-25 minutes on medium heat. Stir to cook evenly.

2. Stir in wine while scraping the bottom of the pan with a flat-sided wooden spoon to deglaze. You want to be sure to get it all – that's where the flavour is.

3. Add broth, stir and then simmer covered for 20 minutes.

4. While soup is simmering, slice bread into ½-inch thick pieces. Measure each fit just inside the rim around the top your oven-proof bowls. Trim as necessary. Turn oven on to broiler setting.

5. Season soup to taste. Ladle into oven-proof bowls. Top each with a slice of bread and then cover the bread generously with fresh grated cheese.

6. Place loaded bowls under broiler for about 3 minutes, or until nicely browned. Be sure to keep an eye on it so your tolling isn't scorched.

7. Remove from oven and serve.

Pasta Fagioli Soup

Ingredients:

3 Tablespoons Olive Oil
2 Medium Onions (Diced)
1 Shallot (finely diced)
3 Cloves Garlic (Minced)
1 - 28 Ounce Tin Diced Tomatoes
6 Cups Water
2-3 Vegetable Broth Cubes
1½ Teaspoons Dried Oregano
1½ Teaspoons Dried Basil
1 Tablespoon Dried Parsley
⅛ - ¼ Teaspoon Cayenne Pepper
1 or 2 pinches Dried Red Pepper Flakes
1 - 19 Ounce Tin Navy Beans
1 - 19 Ounce Tin White Kidney Beans
1 Cup Macaroni (or similar small pasta)
½ Cup Freshly Grated Parmigiano-Reggiano Cheese

Directions:

1. In a small saucepan, boil 3 water and cook
   macaroni according to package instructions.
   Drain, rinse and set aside.

2. In a large stock pot, add olive oil and heat to
   medium. Sauté onions for 3- 4 minutes, then
   stir in minced garlic and cook for a minute
   more.

3. Stir in spices, canned tomatoes, navy beans,
   kidney beans, water and broth cubes. Bring to

a boil, then immediately reduce temperature to low, cover and simmer for 30 minutes, stirring occasionally.

4. Add cooked pasta and ¼ cup grated parmigiano-reggiano and stir well.

5. Season to taste. Ladle into bowls and top each with a sprinkle of the remaining cheese.

Cream of Celery Soup

Ingredients:

3 Tablespoon Olive Oil
2 Tablespoons Butter
2 Medium Onions (chopped fine)
1 Tablespoon Dried Parsley
1-2 Pinches Dried Red Pepper Flakes
4 Cups Water
2 Vegetable Broth Cubes
5-6 Small Potatoes (peeled and diced)
1⅓ heads Celery (chopped)
3 Tablespoons All-Purpose Unbleached Flour
2 Cups Milk

Directions:

1. In a large stock pot, heat 1 tablespoon of olive oil to medium, then add onions and sauté for 3-4 minutes until onions are softened.

2. Add carrots, potatoes, parsley and red pepper flakes and mix well.

3. Stir in water and broth cubes, bring to a boil, then reduce to low, cover and simmer for 1o minutes.

4. Add chopped celery and return to a soft boil, then reduce, cover pot and simmer for another 10 minutes or until celery is tender.

5. While the soup simmers, take a medium saucepan and combine butter with the two remaining tablespoons of olive oil. Heat to medium and add flour. Stir vigorously for about 2 minutes. Add milk a little at a time, while continuing to stir.

6. When heated throughout, pour the thickened milk mixture into soup and mix well.

7. Remove from heat and use an immersion blender to blend soup to desired consistency. Blend it all for a smooth soup, or ⅔- ¾ of the pot for a slightly chunkier version.

8. Season to taste. Ladle into bowls and serve.

French Canadian Pea Soup

Ingredients:

2 Tablespoons Olive Oil
2 Medium Onions (chopped)
3 Cloves Garlic (minced)
2 Stalks Celery (chopped)
2 Medium Carrots (chopped)
2 Bay Leaves
1 Tablespoon Dried Parsley
⅛ Teaspoon Cayenne Pepper
2 Cups Yellow Split Peas
8 Cups Water
3 Vegetable Broth Cubes

Directions:

1. In a large stock pot, heat olive oil to medium and add onions. Cook for 2 minutes, while stirring.

2. Stir in garlic, carrot, and celery and continue to cook for another 3 minutes.

3. Add bay leaves, cayenne pepper, split peas, water and broth cubes and stir. Bring mixture to a boil, then reduce to low, cover and simmer for 2 hours – stirring occasionally. When peas are tender, discard bay leaves.

4. Remove 2 cups of soup and blend. Return
    blended mixture to soup pot and stir
    thoroughly.

5. Season to taste. Ladle into bowls and serve.

Cheddar Vegetable Chowder

Ingredients:

2 Tablespoons Olive Oil
1 Large Onion (finely chopped)
½ Teaspoon Paprika
½ Teaspoon Dried Mustard
½Teaspoon Worcestershire Sauce
2 Large Carrots (sliced)
½ Large Head Cauliflower (chopped into bite-size florets)
½ Bunch Broccoli (chopped into florets)
1 Cup Frozen Peas
1 Cup Frozen Corn
5 Cups Water
2 Vegetable Broth Cubes
3 Tablespoons Butter
⅓ Cup All-Purpose Flour
2 Cups Milk
4 Cups Old Cheddar (Shredded)
Salt and Pepper To Taste

Directions:

1. In a large stock pot, add olive oil and heat to medium. Add onions and sauté for 3 minutes.

2. Add paprika, dried mustard, carrots and cauliflower and stir to coat with oil.

3. Add 2 cups of water, bring it to a boil, then reduce to low, cover and simmer for 15 minutes.

4. Stir in remaining water, broth cubes, peas, corn and broccoli. Return to boil, then reduce to simmer, cover and cook for another 5-7 minutes or until vegetables are tender.

5. In a separate medium-sized saucepan, melt butter, combine with flour and stir continuously for about 2 minutes and then gradually add milk, while continuing to stir mixture.

6. Heat milk mixture to steaming, being careful NOT to boil it. Reduce to simmer and stir in 3 cups of cheese (one handful at a time) until melted and well blended.

7. Combine cheese mixture with soup and stir well.

8. Season to taste. Ladle into bowls and top each bowl with a little extra grated cheese.

Vegetable Barley Soup

Ingredients:

2 Tablespoons Olive Oil
2 Medium Onions (finely diced)
1 Large (or 2 small) Cloves Garlic (minced)
½ Cup Barley
1 Teaspoon Dried Basil
1 Teaspoon Dried Oregano
1-2 Pinches Red Pepper Flakes
2 Medium New Potatoes (diced)
2 Medium Carrots (diced)
8 Cups Water
3 Broth Cubes
½ Head Cauliflower (chopped into bite-size florets)
½ Bunch Broccoli (chopped into bite-size florets)
½ Cup Pasta (tubetti, macaroni, etc.)

Directions:

1. In a small saucepan, boil water and cook pasta according to package instructions. Drain, rinse well and set aside.

2. In a large stock pot, heat olive oil to medium, add onions and sauté for 2-3 minutes. Stir in garlic and sauté mixture for one minute longer.

3. Add spices and barley. Stir well for a minute or two to coat the barley with oil.

4. Stir in water and broth cubes. Bring to a boil, reduce to low, cover and simmer for 15 minutes.

5. Add carrots, potatoes and cauliflower. Return to boil, reduce, cover and simmer another 15 minutes.

6. Add broccoli, peas and corn. Return to boil, reduce and simmer covered for 7-10 minutes lore.

7. Remove 2-3 cups of mostly vegetables (look for large chucks of potatoes and cauliflower) and blend until smooth. Return to stock pot and mix well.

8. Stir in pasta. Season to taste. Ladle into bowls and serve.

Minestrone Soup

Ingredients:

¼ Cup Olive Oil
2 Medium Onions (chopped)
3 Cloves Garlic (minced)
1 Celery Stalk (diced)
2 Medium Carrots (diced)
1 Teaspoon Dried Oregano
2 Teaspoons Dried Basil
1 Tablespoon Dried Parsley
⅛ Teaspoon Cayenne Pepper
9 Cups Water
3-4 Vegetable Broth Cubes
1 – 28 Ounce Tin Diced Tomatoes
2 Medium New Potatoes (diced)
2 Zucchini (Yellow or Green, halved and sliced)
2 Cups Fresh Beans (Green or Yellow, cut to 1 inch)
1 Cup Frozen Peas
1 Large Handful of Baby Spinach (ripped into strips)
1 - 19 Ounce Tin Navy Beans (drained and rinsed)
1 Cup Small Pasta
1 Cup Freshly Grated Parmigiano-Reggiano Cheese

Directions:

1. In a small saucepan, boil water and cook pasta according to package directions. Drain, rinse and set aside.

2. In a large stock pot, heat olive oil to medium and add onions, garlic, carrot and celery and

cook while stirring for about 5 minutes. Add seasonings, stir well and continue to cook for another 2 minutes.

3. Add potatoes, canned tomatoes, water and broth cubes. Bring to a boil, Reduce to low, cover and simmer for 10 minutes.

4. Stir in fresh beans. Return to boil, reduce and simmer covered for another 7 minutes.

5. Add navy beans, zucchini, peas and simmer for 5 minutes.

6. Stir in fresh spinach for another minute or so.

7. Ladle into bowls. Top each bowl with a sprinkling of parmigiano-reggiano and serve.

Lentil and Tomato Soup

Ingredients:

2 Tablespoons Olive Oil
1 Large (or 2 medium) Onions (finely diced)
1 Large Clove Garlic (minced)
½ Teaspoon Ground Ginger
½ Teaspoon Turmeric
½ Teaspoon Coriander
1 Tablespoon Dried Parsley
⅛ Teaspoon Cayenne Pepper
1 Medium Potato (diced)
2 Medium Carrots (chopped)
1⅓ Cups Red Lentils
1 – 28 Ounce Tin Diced Tomatoes
6 Cups Water
3 Vegetable Broth Cubes

Directions:

1. Measure lentils in large measuring cup and rinse thoroughly under cold water and drain. Remove any tiny pebbles or other debris. Set aside.

2. In a large stock pot, heat olive oil to medium, add onion and sauté until softened (about 4 minutes).

3. Add lentils and stir to coat with oil and then add spices while stirring.

4. Add potato, carrot, water, broth cubes and tomatoes. Bring to a boil. Reduce to low. Cover and simmer for about 45 minutes, stirring occasionally.

5. Remove 2 cups, blend until smooth and then return blended mixture to stock pot and mix well.

6. Season to taste. Ladle into bowls and serve.

Potato Leek Soup

Ingredients:

3 Tablespoons Olive Oil
3 Leeks (trimmed ends and most of green tops)
2 Cloves Garlic (minced)
½ Teaspoon Dried Thyme
1 Tablespoon Dried Parsley
¾ Cup Dry White Wine
4 Large Potatoes (peeled and diced)
8 Cups Water
3 Vegetable Broth Cubes

Directions:

1. Cut leeks lengthwise, peel back out layers on green ends, rinse thoroughly under cold water and then slice finely.

2. In a large stock pot, add olive oil and heat to medium. Add sliced leeks, mix well and sauté for 3 minutes.

3. Add garlic and seasonings and cook for an additional two minutes, stirring constantly.

4. Stir in diced potatoes and wine. Mix well. Continue cooking for 2 more minutes.

5. Add water and broth cubes and bring it to a boil, reduce to low, cover and simmer for 15-20 minutes until potatoes are tender.

6. Remove from heat and blend soup in pot using an immersion blender, or transfer to countertop version, blend and return to pot. For a chunkier version, set aside 2 cups of cooked potatoes before blending and stir in afterwards.

7. Season to taste with freshly ground black pepper and salt (if necessary) and serve.

Cream of Fried Potato Soup

Ingredients:

¼ Cup Olive Oil
4-5 Large New Potatoes (cubed into ½-inch pieces)
1 Large Onion (finely diced)
1 Medium Carrot (diced)
1 Celery Stalk (diced)
⅛ Teaspoon Cayenne Pepper
1 Tablespoon Parsley
2 Cups Water
1 Vegetable Broth Cube
6 Tablespoons All-Purpose Unbleached Flour
4 Cups Hot Milk
2 Cups Grated Mozzarella

Directions:

1. In a wide saucepan, add olive oil and heat to medium.

2. Add potatoes, stir to coat with oil and continue frying potatoes. When potatoes are about ½-¾ ready, add diced onion and stir well. Continue frying until potatoes are a nice golden brown color. Add spices.

3. Deglaze pan, if necessary with 2 tablespoons of water and a flat-bottomed wooden spoon.

4. Reduce to low heat and sprinkle in flour over potato/onion mixture – one tablespoon at a time – and mix well.

5. Add remaining water and broth cube. Continue stirring and return to medium heat. Cook for another 5-10 minutes, allowing the cube to completely dissolve.

6. In a separate saucepan, heat milk to steaming and stir it into the soup.

7. Remove from heat and blend the entire mixture.

8. Stir in cheese and return to low temperature to heat throughout.

9. Season to taste. Ladle into bowls and serve.

Corn and Tomato Chowder

Ingredients:

1 Tablespoon Olive Oil
1 Large Onion (diced)
1 Large Garlic Clove (minced)
2 Medium Carrots (chopped)
1 Celery Stalk (chopped)
1 Large Potato (diced)
2 Teaspoons Dried Basil
½ Teaspoon Dried Oregano
½Teaspoon Dried Thyme
1 Bay Leaf
⅛ Teaspoon Cayenne Pepper
1 Red Pepper (cored, seeded and diced)
1 Zucchini (diced)
2 Cups Corn (sliced from cob or frozen)
1 – 28 Ounce Tin Diced Tomatoes
5 Cups Water
2 Vegetable Broth Cubes
3 Tablespoons Butter
⅓ Cup All-Purpose Unbleached Flour
2 Cups Milk

Directions:

1. In a medium-sized saucepan, melt butter and
    add flour. Stir constantly for 2 minutes and
    then slowly add milk, while continuing to stir.
    Heat until steaming and then remove and set
    aside.

2. In a large stock pot, heat olive oil to medium,
    add onions and garlic until nicely softened.

3. Add carrots, celery potato and spices and mix,
    continuing to cook for another 2 minutes.

4. Add water and broth cubes. Bring it to a boil,
    reduce to low, cover and simmer for about 12
    minutes, or until potato and carrot are tender.

5. Stir in red pepper, zucchini and tomatoes.
    Bring it back to a boil, reduce, cover and
    simmer for another 7 minutes

6. Remove bay leaf and discard.

7. Take 2 cups of soup mixture, blend and return
    to stock pot.

8. Add thickened milk mixture and stir to allow
    flavours to blend and simmer on medium low
    for 5 -10 minutes.

9. Season to taste. Ladle into bowls and serve.

Winter Vegetable Soup

Ingredients:

2 Tablespoons Olive Oil
2 Medium Onions (diced)
2 Medium Carrots (cut in half lengthwise and sliced)
2 Large Potatoes (peeled and diced)
½ Full Acorn or Butternut Squash (skin and seeds removed – flesh diced)
½ Teaspoon Dried Thyme
1 Tablespoon Dried Parsley
1 Bay Leaf
5 Cups Water
2 Vegetable Broth Cubes
2 Tablespoons Butter
¼ Cup Flour
1⅓ Cup Milk

Directions:

1. In a small saucepan, melt butter and medium and stir in flour. Continue stirring for 2 minutes and then slowly stir in milk and heat until mixture is steaming. Remove from heat and set aside.

2. In a large saucepan, add olive oil and heat to medium. Add onions and sauté for 4-5 minutes.

3. Add carrots, potatoes, squash and spices and mix thoroughly with onions for 2-3 minutes.

4. Add water and broth cubes, stir and bring to a boil. Reduce to low, cover and simmer for 25 minutes.

5. Remove two cups and blend. Return blended mix and thickened milk mixture to stock pot and stir. Heat throughout.

6. Season to taste. Ladle into bowls and serve.

Vegetable Bean Soup

Ingredients:

2 Tablespoons Olive Oil
1 Large Onion (diced)
1 Celery Stalk (chopped)
2 Medium Carrots (diced)
1 Yellow Pepper (cored, seeded and diced)
10 White or Brown Mushrooms (chopped)
1 Zucchini (diced)
1 Fresh Tomato (cored and diced)
2 large Kale Leaves (shredded)
1 – 19 Ounce Tin White Kidney Beans (drained and rinsed)
1 – 19 Ounce Tin Navy Beans (drained and rinsed)
2 Teaspoons Dried Basil
1 Teaspoon Dried Oregano
¼ Teaspoon Dried Thyme
½ Teaspoon Red Pepper Flakes
1 – 28 Ounce Tin Crushed Tomatoes
6 Cups Water
2 Vegetable Broth Cubes
1 Cup Small Pasta (macaroni, penne, tubetti)
¼ Cup Freshly Grated Parmesan Cheese

Directions:

1. In a small saucepan, boil water and cook pasta according to package instructions. Drain, rinse and set aside.

2. In a large stock pot, heat oil to medium. Add onions, celery and carrots and sauté for about 7 minutes.

3. Add spices, yellow pepper, zucchini, mushrooms and fresh tomato and cook for 5 minutes more. If it gets too dry, add a splash of water and stir.

4. Add water and broth cubes. Bring it to a boil, reduce to low, cover and simmer for 5-7 minutes.

5. Stir in crushed tomatoes, white kidney beans and navy beans and return to boil, reduce, cover and simmer for about 10 minutes.

6. Stir in kale for another couple of minutes and add pre-cooked pasta and mix soup well.

7. Season to taste. Ladle into bowls and serve.

Grilled Vegetable Soup

Ingredients:

3 Tablespoons Olive Oil
2 Cloves Garlic (minced)
1 Bunch of Asparagus (woody ends removed, remainder sliced into 1½- inch pieces)
1 Red + 2 Yellow Bell Peppers (cored, seeded and chopped into large chunks)
1 Red Onion (medium diced)
1 Zucchini (sliced)
6 Large Mushrooms (quartered)
10 Brussels Sprouts (trimmed and sliced into 3 or 4 pieces)
1 Teaspoon Dried Basil
½ Teaspoon Dried Oregano
½ Teaspoon Turmeric
⅛ Teaspoon Cayenne Pepper
1 Tablespoon Dried Parsley
Freshly Ground Sea Salt and Pepper
7 Cups Water
3 Vegetable Broth Cubes
1 – 28 Ounce Tin Diced Tomatoes

Directions:

1. In a large mixing bowl, place prepared asparagus, bell peppers, red onion, zucchini, mushrooms and brussels sprouts. Combine with olive oil and minced garlic. Add freshly-ground salt and pepper. Let stand for 30-60 minutes, stirring periodically.

2. Fire up the BBQ. Spray a grilling basket with olive oil or cooking spray to prevent sticking and grill the vegetables on medium heat. Toss occasionally so they cook evenly. Cook until vegetables are softened, with grill marks on most of the pieces. This typically takes 15-25 minutes but you'll need to monitor grilling time to suit.

3. When veggies are ready, turn off the BBQ and place grilled vegetables in a large mixing bowl.

4. In a large stock pot, combine water, broth cubes, canned tomatoes and spices and stir. Bring to a boil, add all the grilled vegetables, reduce to low, cover and simmer for 15-20 minutes.

5. Season to taste. Ladle into bowls and serve.

Hot Potato and Pepper Soup

Ingredients:

¼ Cup Olive Oil
6 Large Potatoes (peeled and cubed into ½-inch pieces)
1 Red Bell Pepper + 2 Yellow (cored, seeded and diced)
8 Cups Water
3-4 Vegetable Broth Cubes
3 Green Onions (Sliced fine)
½ Teaspoon Turmeric
½ Teaspoon Paprika
¼ Teaspoon Cayenne Pepper

Directions:

1. In a wide-bodied saucepan, add half the oil and heat to medium, then add half the potatoes and fry until golden brown. Toss frequently to cook evenly and minimize sticking.

2. Set aside potatoes in a bowl when they're done. Scrap the pot with a flat-bottomed wooden spoon and save the scrapings with the potatoes.

3. Add remaining oil and potatoes and repeat the
    process until all potatoes are a nice golden
    brown color on the outside.

4. Once the second batch of potatoes is done,
    add a little water and carefully scrap the
    bottom of the pan again.

5. Combine remaining water, broth cubes, diced
    peppers and fried potatoes. Bring to a boil,
    reduce, cover and simmer for 15-20 minutes.

6. Add green onion and simmer for 5 minutes
    more.

7. Season to taste. Ladle into bowls and serve.

Couscous and Mixed Vegetable Soup

Ingredients:

3 Tablespoons Olive Oil
2 Cloves Garlic (minced)
1 Cup Whole Wheat Couscous
½ Teaspoon Red Pepper Flakes
2 Medium Carrots (chopped)
½ Head of Cauliflower (Chopped into bite-size florets)
10 Brussels Sprouts (trimmed and sliced into 3-4 pieces each)
5 Green Onions (chopped)
8 Cups Water
3 Vegetable Broth Cubes

Directions:

1. In a large stock pot, heat oil to medium, add garlic, and cook gently for 1 minute. Add carrots, cauliflower and brussels sprouts, coat with oil and garlic and cook for 5 minutes, stirring frequently.

2. Add water, broth cubes, red pepper flakes and bring mixture to a boil. Reduce to low, cover and simmer for 10 minutes or until vegetables are nearly ready.

3. Stir in couscous and green onions and simmer for another 5 minutes, or so.

4. Season to taste. Ladle into bowls and serve.

Broccoli and Pasta Soup

Ingredients:

2 Tablespoons Olive Oil
2 Medium Onions (diced)
2 Large Cloves Garlic (minced)
1 Large Head Broccoli (cut into bite-size florets, trim, peel and julienne stems)
2 Medium Carrots (diced)
1 Yellow Zucchini (chopped)
⅛ Teaspoon Cayenne Pepper
½ Teaspoon Worcestershire Sauce
8 Cups Water
3-4 Vegetable Broth Cubes
⅙ Standard Package of Angel Hair Pasta (broken into 2-inch pieces)
½ Cup Freshly Grated Parmigiano-Reggiano

Directions:

1. In a large stock pot, add olive oil and heat to medium. Add onions and sauté for 3-4 minutes.

2. Stir in carrots and garlic and cook for another 3 minutes.

3. Add broccoli, zucchini and seasonings and bring it to a boil, reduce to low, cover and simmer for 7-10 minutes or until broccoli reaches desired tenderness.

4. Add angel hair and stir. Cook for about 3 minutes and check pasta. If it's not quite done, leave it for another minute or so. (Angel hair tends to cook fast.)

5. Season to taste. Ladle into bowls, top each with a sprinkling of Parmigiano-Reggiano and serve.

Cream of Broccoli Soup

Ingredients:

2 Tablespoons Olive Oil
2 Medium Onions (chopped)
3 Cloves Garlic (minced)
1 Celery Stalk (diced)
1 Medium Carrot (diced)
2 Medium New Potatoes (chopped into ½-inch squares)
2 Heads Broccoli (cut into bite-size florets, stems trimmed, peeled and chopped)
1 Teaspoon Worcestershire Sauce
⅛ Teaspoon Cayenne Pepper
4 Cups Water
2 Vegetable Broth Cubes
3 Tablespoons Butter
⅓ Cup All-Purpose Unbleached Flour
2 Cups Milk

Directions:

1. In a large stock pot, heat olive oil to medium, add onions and sauté for 3 minutes. Add minced garlic and continue for one minute more.

2. Add carrots and celery and stir. Cook for another 5-7 minutes or until celery has softened somewhat.

3. Add water, broth cubes, seasonings and
    potato. Bring pot to a boil, reduce to low, cover
    and simmer for 12 minutes, then add all
    broccoli and return to boil, reduce, cover and
    simmer for another 10 minutes.

4. Remove from heat, blend soup and then return
    to pan.

5. In a separate, medium-sized saucepan, melt
    the butter on medium heat and stir in flour.
    This should make a thick paste. If too dry, add
    a splash of olive oil and cook for 2 minutes
    while stirring. Slowly add milk and heat to
    steaming.

6. Combine milk mixture with soup and heat
    throughout.

7. Season to taste. Ladle into bowls and serve.

Lentil and Pasta Soup

Ingredients:

3 Tablespoons Olive Oil
2 Medium Onions (diced)
2 Medium Carrots (chopped)
2 Celery Stalks (chopped)
1½ Cup Red Lentils (rinsed)
¾ Teaspoon Crushed Red Pepper Flakes
8 Cups Water
3 Vegetable Broth Cubes
1 Cup Dried Pasta (macaroni works well)
½ Cup Freshly Grated Parmigiano-Reggiano Cheese

Directions:

1. In large stock pot, heat oil to medium and sauté onions for 3 minutes. Stir in garlic, carrots, celery and red pepper flakes and cook for another 5 minutes.

2. Stir in lentils and mix well.

3. Add water and broth cubes, bring to a boil, reduce to low, cover and simmer for 7 minutes.

4. Stir in dried pasta, return to boil, reduce, cover and simmer for 10 minutes more, or until pasta is just right.

5. Season to taste. Ladle into bowls, top each
    serving with parmigiano-reggiano and serve.

Corn Chowder

Ingredients:

2 Tablespoons Olive Oil
2 Medium Onions (finely diced)
1 Clove Garlic (minced)
1 Medium Carrot (diced)
2 Medium potatoes (peeled and diced)
1 Jalapeno Pepper (cored, seeded and finely diced)
1 Cup Fresh Green Peas
4 Cups Fresh Corn Kernels
1 Bay Leaf
4 Cups Water
2 Vegetable Broth Cubes
3 Tablespoons Butter
⅓ Cup Flour
2 Cups Milk

Directions:

1. In a large stock, heat olive oil to medium, add onions and sauté for 3 minutes and then add garlic and jalapeno and continue for another 2 minutes or so.

2. Stir in carrots and potato. Mix well to coat with onion/garlic/jalapeno mixture.

3. Add water, broth cubes and bay leaf and bring to a boil. Reduce to low, cover and simmer for 12-15 minutes.

4. Add corn and peas, return to boil, reduce and simmer for about 10 minutes - or until corn and peas are tender.

5. Remove 2 cups and blend. Then return to stock pot.

6. In a separate, medium-sized saucepan, melt butter at medium heat and stir in flour for 2 minutes. Slowly add milk and heat to steaming, then remove and add milk to vegetable mixture. Mix well and heat throughout.

7. Season to taste. Ladle into bowls and serve.

Bean and Salsa Soup

Ingredients:

2 Tablespoons Olive Oil
2 Cloves Garlic (minced)
1 Red and 1 Yellow Bell Pepper (cored, seeded and quartered)
1 Medium Onion
1 Medium Carrot (diced)
1 Celery Stalk (diced)
2 Cups Salsa
2 Cups Water
1 Vegetable Broth Cube
1 – 19 Ounce Tin Red Kidney Beans (drained and rinsed)
1 – 19 Ounce Tin Black Beans (drained and rinsed)
1 – 19 Ounce Tin White Kidney Beans (drained and rinsed)
¼ Teaspoon Dried Marjoram
⅛ Teaspoon Dried Thyme
⅛ Teaspoon Cayenne Pepper
3 Green Onions (finely chopped)
½ Cup Sour Cream or Greek Yogurt

Directions:

1. Preheat oven to 350 degrees Fahrenheit.

2. In a mixing bowl, combine 1 tablespoon of olive oil, garlic and quartered peppers, coating both sides of peppers.

3. Place peppers on a shallow roasting pan (skin side down) and roast for 12-15 minutes. Flip peppers and roast for another 12 minutes.

4. Remove peppers from oven and let cool. Chop into smaller pieces and set aside.

5. In a large saucepan, heat remaining tablespoon of olive oil to medium and add onions, celery, carrot and spices and cook gently for about 5 minutes.

6. Stir in water and broth cube, bring to a boil, reduce to low, cover and simmer for 7 minutes.

7. Add beans, salsa and reserved peppers. Stir well and heat throughout.

8. Puree half of the mixture until smooth and return to saucepan and mix well.

9. Season to taste. Ladle into bowls and top each serving with a little sour cream or Greek yogurt. Then sprinkle a few diced green onions on top and serve.

Cream of Cauliflower Soup

Ingredients:

2 Tablespoons Olive Oil
2 Medium Onions (diced)
1 Celery Stalk (diced)
1 Medium Carrot (diced)
1 Large New Potato (chopped)
1 Large Head Cauliflower (chopped into florets and small stem pieces)
4 Cups Water
2 Vegetable Broth Cubes
3 Tablespoons Butter
⅓ Cup All-Purpose Unbleached Flour
2 Cups Milk
½ Teaspoon Worcestershire Sauce
½ Teaspoon Dried Mustard
⅛ Teaspoon Cayenne Pepper
1 Cup Fresh Grated Swiss Cheese
2 Tablespoons Fresh Chives (chopped)

Directions:

1. In a large stock pot, heat olive oil to medium, add onions, celery and carrots and sauté for 5 minutes.

2. Add water, broth cubes, seasonings, potato and cauliflower and stir. Bring to boil, reduce to low, cover and simmer for 15 minutes, or until potato and cauliflower is tender.

3. If you prefer a chunkier version, set aside 1½
    of cooked cauliflower florets, then return after
    blending.

4. Puree soup in stock pot with an immersion
    blender, or remove a few cups at a time, blend
    using a standard blender, then return.

5. In a separate saucepan, melt butter on
    medium heat, mix in flour and stir continuously
    for 2 minutes. Slowly stir in milk and heat until
    steaming and add milk mixture to stock pot.

6. Stir in freshly grated cheese mix well.

7. Season to taste. Ladle into bowls, top each
    with a sprinkling of fresh chives and serve.

Roasted Butternut Squash Soup

Ingredients:

2 Tablespoons Olive Oil
1 Tablespoon Butter
2 Medium Onions (diced)
2 Large Butternut Squash (or 4 Small)
8 Cups Water
3 Vegetable Broth Cubes
1 Teaspoon Dried Marjoram
2 Teaspoons Dried Parsley
2 – 8 Ounce Packages Cream Cheese

Directions:

1. Preheat oven to 375 degrees Fahrenheit.

2. Wash Squash and pat dry. Slice along the entire length and remove seeds and stringy flesh. Place squash halves in a large roasting pan filled with about ½ inch of water. Bake at 375F for 45 minutes.

3. Remove squash from oven and allow it to cool. Once cooled, remove outer skin and then chop squash into small pieces.

4. In a large stock pot, heat olive oil and butter to medium. Add onions and sauté for 5 minutes.

5. Add water, broth cubes, seasonings and roasted squash and stir. Bring to a boil, reduce to low, cover and simmer for about 10 minutes.

6. Stir in cream cheese – a little at a time – and mix well.

7. Blend all contents into a smooth consistency.

8. Season to taste. Ladle into bowls and serve.

Cheesy Potato and Cauliflower Soup

Ingredients:

1 Tablespoon Olive Oil
1 Medium Onion (diced)
2 Cloves Garlic (minced)
2 Medium Carrots (chopped)
6 Medium New Potatoes (diced)
1 head cauliflower (chopped into bite-size pieces)
6 Cups Water
3 Vegetable Broth Cubes
¼ Teaspoon Dried Dill
¼ Teaspoon Cayenne Pepper
3 Tablespoons Butter
⅓ Cup Flour
2 Cups Milk
2 Cups Grated Cheddar (or mixed blend) Cheese

Directions

1. In a small saucepan, melt butter on medium, stir in flour and mix for 2 minutes. Slowly add milk while continually stirring. When mixed, remove from heat and set aside.

2. In a large stock pot, add olive oil, heat to medium and add onions. Sauté for about 3 minutes, add garlic and cook for another minute.

3. Stir in carrots, potatoes and cauliflower and mix well. Add water and broth cubes. Bring to a boil, reduce to low, cover and simmer for 20 minutes.

4. Blend soup and return to stock pot.

5. Stir in reserved milk mixture, cheese and seasonings. Allow to simmer for 10 minutes or until heated throughout and flavours well-blended.

6. Season to taste. Ladle into bowls and serve.

Sweet Potato, Roasted Garlic and Kale Soup

Ingredients:

Roasted Garlic
2 small-medium heads of garlic
Splash of olive oil
Freshly ground sea salt and pepper

Soup
1 Tablespoon Olive Oil
I Medium Onion (finely diced)
I Medium Carrot (chopped)
1 Large Sweet Potato (peeled and diced)
1 Medium New Potato (diced)
1 – 19 Ounce Tin White Kidney Beans
8 Cups Water
3 Vegetable Broth Cubes
½ Teaspoon Dried Thyme
½ Teaspoon Dried Basil
1 Teaspoon Dried Parsley
⅛ Teaspoon Cayenne Pepper
½ Large Bunch Fresh Kale (chopped fine leafy greens)
2 Green Onions (chopped fine)
1 Cup Pasta (shells, macaroni, or fusilli works well)

Directions:

1. Preheat oven to 400 degrees Fahrenheit.

2. Slice off the top of each head of garlic –just
    enough to expose flesh.

3. Take two small squares of aluminum foil
    Drizzle a little olive oil and add a sprinkle of
    salt and pepper. Place garlic (cut side down)
    on foil then wrap it. Roast for 45 minutes.

4. Remove garlic from oven and place in a small
    bowl and allow it to cool. Once cooled, discard
    the outer skin and ends and return the fleshly
    segments to the bowl and mash.

5. In a small saucepan, cook pasta according to
    package instructions. Drain, rinse and set
    aside.

6. In a large stock pot, heat olive oil to medium
    and sauté onion for 4 minutes

7. Add carrot, potato, sweet potato and
    seasonings and mix. Stir in water and broth
    cubes. Bring to a boil, reduce to low, cover and
    simmer for about 15 minutes, or until
    vegetables are tender.

8. Stir in beans and mashed garlic. Mix well and
    heat throughout.

9. On low heat, stir in chopped kale, green onions
    and pasta and simmer for a few minutes more.

10. Season to taste. Ladle into bowls and serve.

Cream of Vegetable Soup

Ingredients:

2 Tablespoons Olive Oil
2 Medium Onions, diced
4 large Garlic Cloves, minced
1 large head of Cauliflower, chopped into bite-size pieces
1 large Potato, scrubbed and diced
1 large Red Pepper, diced
1 bunch of fresh, green Asparagus, sliced into 1-inch pieces
4 cups of vegetable broth
2 Tablespoon Butter (for blending with flour and milk)
2 Tablespoons of Whole Wheat Flour
1 – 11/2 cups of Milk
½ teaspoon of ground Black Pepper
Pinch of Sea Salt
¼ teaspoon of ground Nutmeg
½ Tablespoon of dried Parsley
2 cups of Swiss Cheese, grated (optional)

Directions:

6. In a large stock pot, add olive oil and heat to medium. Add onions and sauté for 2-3 minutes. Then add minced garlic and cook for another minute.

7. Add diced potato, red pepper and cauliflower and cook while stirring for about 5 minutes.

8. Add vegetable broth and increase to high heat. As soon as it begins to boil, cover with lid, reduce heat to low and set your timer for 12 minutes. Do not lift the lid during this time.

9. Add asparagus and seasonings and mix thoroughly. Bring heat back up to high, then cover and reduce to low for about 5 minutes, or until the asparagus is tender.

10. In a separate small pot, melt butter and add flour. Stir vigorously for about a minute. Continue stirring as you add the milk a little at a time.

11. Place ⅓ to ½ of the soup in a large mixing bowl and blend it using an immersion blender, or use your counter-top blender if you prefer. Return blended soup to pot. This produces a soup that is thick and creamy (without the cream) and yet it still has nice chunks of vegetables. If you prefer, you can blend the entire thing.

12. Add thickened milk mixture to soup and stir well.

13. Stir in grated cheese (if using), season to taste and serve.

Cream of Potato with Dill Soup

Ingredients:

2 Tablespoons Olive Oil
2 medium or 1 large Onion, diced
2 carrots, peeled and diced
2 stalks of Celery, diced
5 large Potatoes, peeled and diced
4 cups of Vegetable Broth
3 Tablespoons of Butter
1 Tablespoon Olive Oil (to be combined with butter)
¼ cup of Whole Wheat Flour
2 Cups of Milk
2 teaspoons of dried Parsley
½ teaspoon of ground Black Pepper
½ to ¾ teaspoon of dried Dill (depending on your taste preferences)

Directions:

1. In a large stock pot, heat olive oil to medium and add diced onions, carrots and celery. Sauté this mix for about 3-4 minutes or until vegetables become slightly tender.
2. Stir in potato, coating each piece with a little of the oil. Continue for about 5 minutes.

3. Add vegetable broth to the stock pot and stir it in. Increase the temperature to high until the mixture begins to boil. Cover and reduce heat

to low heat. Leave the cover on for about 15 minutes until diced potatoes have softened.

4. While potatoes are cooking, place a small sauce pan on medium-high heat and combine the 3 tablespoons of butter with the 1 tablespoon of olive oil. Stir continuously for about one minute before slowly adding the milk a little bit at a time and stirring as you do so.

5. Once thickened milk is well mixed and hot throughout, set aside.

6. When potatoes have cooked, remove ⅓ to ½ of the potato soup mixture, blend it and then return the blended soup to your stock pot.
7. Add thickened milk mixture to the soup and stir it to blend well.

8. Mix in the dried dill and other seasonings. Remove stock pot from heat and let it cool a little before serving.

Broccoli and Bean Soup

Ingredients:

2 Tablespoons of Olive Oil
2 medium Onions (diced)
1 large or 2 medium Carrots (diced)
2 stalks of Celery (diced)
½ head of Cauliflower (broken into bite-size pieces)
8 cups of Vegetable Broth
1 large head of Broccoli (broken or chopped into bite-size pieces)
1 tin (19 oz.) of White Kidney Beans or Chick Peas (rinsed)
1-2 pinches of dried red pepper flakes
1-2 pinches of Sea Salt
1 teaspoon Worcestershire Sauce

Directions:

1. In a large stock pot, heat olive oil to medium and add diced onions, carrots and celery. Sauté until slightly softened – for about 3-4 minutes while stirring.

2. Add chopped cauliflower and stir well into the mix for another 2 minutes or so.

3. Add dried red pepper flakes and sea salt.

4. Pour in all vegetable broth and stir well. Bring to a boil. Cover and reduce to low heat for 10 minutes.

5. Add white beans, broccoli florets and
   Worcestershire Sauce and stir to mix well.
   Leave covered on a low-heat simmer for about
   10 minutes, or until broccoli is slightly tender —
   but not overcooked.

6. Adjust seasonings to taste and serve.

Potato Broccoli and Carrot Soup

Ingredients:

¼ cup of Olive Oil
5 medium Potatoes (peeled and chopped to half-inch size pieces)
2 medium Onions (diced)
5 medium-sized cloves of Garlic (minced)
2 large Carrots (halved and sliced)
8 cups of Vegetable Broth
2 small to medium-sized heads of Broccoli (cut into florets, stalks peeled and sliced)
2 teaspoons of Worcestershire Sauce
2-3 pinches of Dried Red Pepper Flakes

Directions:

1. In a large stock pot, heat olive oil to medium and add chopped potatoes. Fry potatoes while constantly tossing with a flat-bottomed spoon or spatula so potatoes don't stick. Cook for about 7 minutes, or until potatoes begin to brown.

2. Add diced onions and minced garlic to the potatoes and continuously toss mix until onions are soft and translucent.

3. Add dried red pepper flakes.

4. Add sliced broccoli stalks and chopped carrots
   and continue cooking while stirring for another
   3 or 4 minutes.

5. Pour vegetable broth into the stock pot. Bring
   it to a boil. Add broccoli florets and
   Worcestershire sauce and stir well. Cover and
   simmer until broccoli is slightly tender, but still
   a bright green color.

6. Season to taste and serve.

Mushroom, Leek and Onion Soup

Ingredients:

3 Tablespoons of Butter
1 Tablespoon of Olive Oil
1 medium onion (diced)
1 medium leek (diced)
1 large, plump clove of garlic (minced)
1 small package of button Mushrooms (cleaned and trimmed, large ones sliced in half or quartered)
1 small package of Shitake Mushrooms (cleaned and sliced)
½ cup of dry White Wine
7 cups of Vegetable Broth
1 ½ cups of fresh, Baby Spinach (chopped)
½ teaspoon of ground Black Pepper
3-4 fresh Green Onions (chopped)

Directions:

1. In a large stock pot, melt butter at medium heat and combine with olive oil. Add diced onion and leeks and continue to stir for about 2 minutes until slightly softened.

2. Stir in minced garlic and black pepper.

3. Add shitake and button mushrooms and cook while stirring continuously for 4-5 minutes.

4. Add white wine and stir well. Allow it to cook
    down for a couple of minutes.

5. Pour vegetable broth into stock pot and bring it
    to a boil.

6. Add chopped spinach. Reduce to low heat,
    cover and simmer for 5 minutes.

7. Stir well and then add chopped green onion.

8. Season to taste and serve.

Faster French Onion Soup

Ingredients:

¼ cup of Olive Oil
10 Large Onions (peeled and thinly sliced)
¼ to ½ teaspoon of Dried Red Pepper Flakes
1 cup of dry White Wine
8 cups of Vegetable Broth
3 Whole Wheat or Multi-Grain Bagels (day old is best
– toasted, cooled and chopped into croutons)
3 cups of grated Swiss cheese

Directions:

1. In a large stock pot, bring olive oil to medium heat.

2. Add all sliced onions and gently fry while stirring. This usually takes about 15-20 minutes to fry the onions to a deep, dark brown color.

3. Add red pepper flakes and mix throughout.

4. Add white wine to deglaze stock pot. Use a flat-bottomed wooden spoon to scrape up all the bits of onion and brown color on the bottom – that's where the flavor is.

5. Once the wine has reduced to about 50%, add all of the stock. Bring it to a boil, then cover and simmer for 5 minutes.

6. Spoon soup into bowls, making sure to get a
    good mix of broth and onion.

7. Sprinkle bagel croutons on top, followed by the
    grated Swiss cheese.

8. Serve and enjoy!

Thank You for Joining Me
on This Soup-Making Journey!

From my kitchen to yours, thank you for taking the time to explore these recipes. It's my hope that these soups become a comforting and delicious part of your life - whether you're sharing them with loved ones or savoring a quiet bowl all to yourself.

Cooking is such a beautiful way to connect, nourish, and create memories, and I'm truly grateful to have shared this little piece of my kitchen with you.

Wishing you warmth, flavor, and countless cozy moments ahead. Enjoy these soups often, and may every pot bring joy to your table!

With heartfelt gratitude,

Susan Scott